Dog

...on th   ....st

The essential guide for dogs and their
owners visiting the North Norfolk Coast

Steve & Alyson Appleyard

Published in 2013 by Red Flannel Publishing

Plumtree House, Mill Lane, East Runton

Norfolk NR27 9PH

ISBN 978-0-9561346-5-3

Sheringham
West Runton
East Runton
Cromer
Overstrand
Mundesley
Bacton
Walcott
Happisburgh
Sea Palling
Waxham
Horsey Gap
Winterton o

Holkham
Wells next the Sea
Stiffkey
Morston
Blakeney
Cley next the Sea
Weybourne

Thornham
Brancaster
Burnham Deepdale
Burnham Overy Staithe

Hunstanton
Heacham
Snettisham

Contents

Introduction

We believe that the North Norfolk Coast is second to none, as both an area to live and as a holiday destination. If you own a dog then it is even more incomparable and we have tried to show you why in this book.

The widely varying coastline makes for very varied walks, from beaches to cliffs and from marshland to pine forest. Dogs are excluded from the busiest holiday beaches in the summer, but this accounts for less than two percent of the coastline and they are crowded places best avoided anyway.

As you will see, many cafés, restaurants and pubs positively welcome dogs - knowing which they are, will make your time here even more enjoyable.

During your stay we recommend that you purchase a book of tidetables, as knowing the state of the tide will both ensure you are walking on the beach at the best times and could prevent you from being cut off by the sea.

Snettisham is the first place on the Wash, heading north from King's Lynn, which has a beach. At low water the tide recedes a great distance but it is much too muddy to venture out. There is a path which leads south to an RSPB reserve and dogs should be kept under close control so as not to disturb the birds. You can walk northwards from the car park along the beach, all the way to Heacham, although it can be hard going on the shingly beach. The car park also leads directly on to a grassy area parallel with the beach, which is also popular with dog walkers. During the summer there are cafe's with outdoor tables at both Snettishm and Heacham, but it is well worth driving inland from Heacham on the B1454 to the King William IV country inn.

There are two beaches at Heacham designated North and South. North Beach has the larger car park and a promenade to walk along. You can walk along the sandy beaches and there is also a path alongside the Heacham River, which runs parallel to the beach. The tide goes out along way and while it is not as muddy as at Snettisham, great care should be taken if you venture out at low water.

The King William IV Country Inn & Restaurant
Heacham Road, Sedgeford
PE36 5LU
"We have a dog friendly bar/restaurant area and a dog friendly garden. Dogs must be kept on leads at all times".
Open all year.

Heacham

The Boat House Cafe

South Beach Road PE36 5BA

(At the southern end of the promenade)

"We don't allow dogs in when very busy ie summer time weekends. We only allow well behaved dogs.

Dogs are allowed at the tables on the seaview decking area".

Closed midweek in winter.

Café Blah Blah

72 Westgate PE36 5EP

(next door to the Sainsbury supermarket)

Dogs allowed without restriction

Tables outside

Open all the year

Hunstanton

Dogs are excluded from the bathing beach from 1st April to 31st October. They should also be kept on a lead while on the promenade adjacent to the bathing beach. The extent of the bathing beach is shown on the beach information boards, but is basically the area within the nineteen groynes.

Hunstanton is a popular holiday resort with beaches and promenade that can become quite crowded in the summer. While there are prohibitions on dogs for the beaches closest to the town, there are no restrictions on the beaches both north and south of this. You can take dogs on to the beach immediately south of the Boat House Cafe (opposite) - and walk towards Heacham. Although Hunstanton is on the east coast of England, it actually faces west and the sunsets over the sea can be spectacular.

The Lighthouse Cafe

Lighthouse Close PE36 6EL
By the Cliff car park
"Dogs are welcome inside the
cafe and on the outside benches.
Dog water is provided as well as
a dog biscuit" .
Open - April to October inclusive
Weekends December - March.
February half term
Boxing day - to New Year's Day

The Rendezvous

13 High Street PE36 5AB
"Dogs allowed inside on leads"
Open all the year

Dogs are allowed on the beach at any time beyond the end of the North Promenade and the most northerly of the groynes. At low water you can walk around the headland towards Old Hunstanton. The distinctive cliffs are made up of three contrasting rock strata - white and red chalk and Carrstone. The bottom view is from the Lighthouse cafe, looking northwards to the beach at Old Hunstanton.

The Old Boathouse Cafe

50 Sea Lane PE36 6J
As can be seen in the photograph, the
Old Boathouse Cafe is virtually on the
beach at Old Hunstanton.
There are tables outside in the
summer and as the sign says -
"dogs on leads are welcome inside" -
and their Facebook page says -
"even wet smelly ones".
Open all the year -
Thursday to Sunday.

Le Strange Old Barns

While in Old Hunstanton we can
recommend a visit to Le Strange Old
Barns - Antiques, Arts and Crafts
centre. You pass it on the way down
to the beach. Dogs are not permitted
inside, but we're sure they won't mind
waiting in the car while you pop inside.

The delightful uncommercialised beach at Old Hunstanton is owned by the Le Strange family - who were responsible for creation of the "new" Hunstanton. According to the beach information board there are no restrictions on dogs at any time of the year, but do be aware that it can be quite busy in the summer holidays. There is a beach car park which is a short walk from the beach and a right turn off this track leads to an area on the landward side of the sand dunes, which is popular for walking dogs.

13

La Campagna
(Restaurant in a yurt)
Drove Orchards PE36 6LS
"Dogs allowed during the daytime
(10-4 winter, 9-5 summer)
- with well behaved humans on
leads!"
Not allowed inside during the
evening service.
Open all year. Tables outside

The Orange Tree
High Street PE36 6LY
"Dogs allowed in the bar area and
in the guest rooms. Only allowed
to eat off the dog menu!"
Many outdoor tables
Open all year
Norfolk dining pub of the year -
The Good Pub Guide 2013

From the small carpark by the creek at Thornham you can walk along a path on a raised embankment to an extensive sandy beach. The area comprises part of the Norfolk Wildlife Trust's Holme Dunes Reserve and the NWT draws attention to the Coastal Code with respect to dogs

"Avoid disturbing birds and animals - birds using the beach and dunes are at risk. Keep your dog under tight control. Wildlife, livestock and other people can feel threatened by dogs."

Brancaster is a popular beach in the summer, renowned for its wide expanse of firm sand at low water. You can walk along the beach, alternatively the Norfolk Coast Path passes through Brancaster at the village end of the beach road. In an easterly direction the path follows the edge of the marshes for $1\frac{1}{4}$ miles to Brancaster Staithe. The westerly Coast Path actually goes inland for one mile before then heading west for $1\frac{1}{2}$ miles and then turning north to Thornham.

There is a large pay and display carpark at the beach, which is not free to National Trust members, even though the surrounding area is owned by the Trust.

 There is a triangular shaped area of the beach which has a summer restriction, this is shown on the beach information board. No dogs are allowed in this area between 1st May and 15th September. If you wish to walk along the beach further to the west of this area, you must access it by the footpath to the landward side of the golf course club house.

The Ship Hotel
Main Road PE31 8AP
"Dogs are allowed in all public areas
excluding our restaurant.
We also allow dogs in six of
our nine bedrooms."
Outdoor tables
Open all year

Burnham Deepdale is on the edge of the marshes with no access to the beach.

Brancaster Staithe is one mile west and Burnham Overy Staithe $3^3/_4$ miles east on the Norfolk Coast Path. A limited amount of roadside parking.

Deepdale Café
Main Road PE31 8DD
"Dogs are welcome in our cafe as long as they are dry, quietly spoken and better behaved than their owners"
Outdoor Tables

Deeepdale Backpackers & Camping
Main Road PE31 8NW
"Dogs allowed - must be kept on a lead on the campsite
We have two dog friendly yurts and two dog friendly tipis and one dog friendly room.

The Hoste
The Green

Burnham Market PE31 8HD

"Dogs are very welcome in our bar where there is a water bowl - and in the conservatory. Dogs can stay in the rooms with resident guests""

Outdoor tables

Tilly's Cafe
The Green, Market Place

Burnham Market PE31 8HF

"We allow dogs inside on the six tables furthest from the kitchen. We are always pleased to welcome well behaved dogs. A small treat is often available and a water bowl is outside."

The Nelson
Creake Road

Burnham Market PE31 8EN

"Dogs are welcome in the bar area"

Outdoor tables

Burnham Overy Staithe is more than one mile inland from the sea on the tidal Overy Creek.

The car park alongside the creek can get very busy in the summer.

The walk along the raised embankment to the beach, which is the route of the Norfolk Coast Path, provides panoramic views of the creek and saltings to your left, grazing marshes to your right and the picturesque quayside behind you. Finally your arrive at a large ridge of sand dunes, beyond which is a superb expanse of beach. You can follow the beach and the Coast Path eastwards for a further two miles to Holkham.

You are within the Holkham National Nature Reserve and should avoid the dunes and be aware of ground nesting birds.

19

Holkham

Rose Garden Café
Main Road Holkham Village

NR23 1AD

(Directly off the A149)

"All dogs are allowed in the
gardens and well behaved dogs
are allowed in the cafe!"

Outdoor tables

Open all year - except Christmas

The Victoria Hotel
Park Road Holkham Village

NR23 1RG

"Dogs are welcome in all areas
apart from the restaurant"

Three bedrooms suitable for dogs

Outdoor tables

Open all year

(Note - closed for refurbishment
until early May 2013)

The beach and the bay at Holkham are at the centre of the Holkham National Nature Reserve, which stretches from Burnham Norton to Blakeney and covers some 4000 hectares

You have a wide choice of walking here, the beach, within the pine trees or the Norfolk Coast path. The Coast path westwards follows the border between the pine trees and the beach and then the beach and the dunes, to Burnham Overy Staithe, a distance of around $3\frac{1}{2}$ miles. Our favourite is a circular walk, initially following the Coast path westwards (this is on the landward side of the trees) to Wells lifeboat station and then return along the beach. This is a total distance of about four miles and you can stop half way for refreshments at the Beach Cafe.

There is car parking in Lady Ann's Drive, which is directly off the A149 opposite the main entrance to Holkham Hall.

While walking anywhere within this area you should remember that it is a nature reserve and dogs should be kept under close control.

21

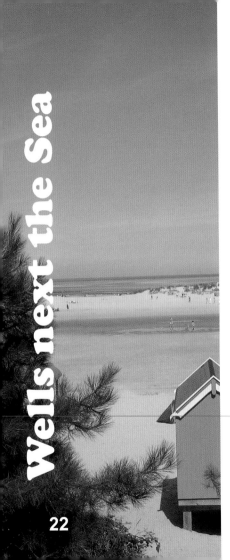

Beach Café

Beach Road NR23 1DR

"In the winter months after a
bracing walk on the beach, get comfy
in our sofas and arm chairs around
the warmth of the roaring
wood-burning stove. Your four-legged
friends are welcome inside too!"

The Globe Inn

The Buttlands NR23 1EU

"Dogs allowed in downstairs bar area"
Three rooms available for dogs
Tables in outside courtyard area

The Edinburgh Inn

(Ollie's Restaurant)
Station Road NR23 1AE

"Dogs allowed in all the bar areas and
half of the seating/food area".
Dog friendly beer garden
Pub open all year - restaurant closed
in November and January

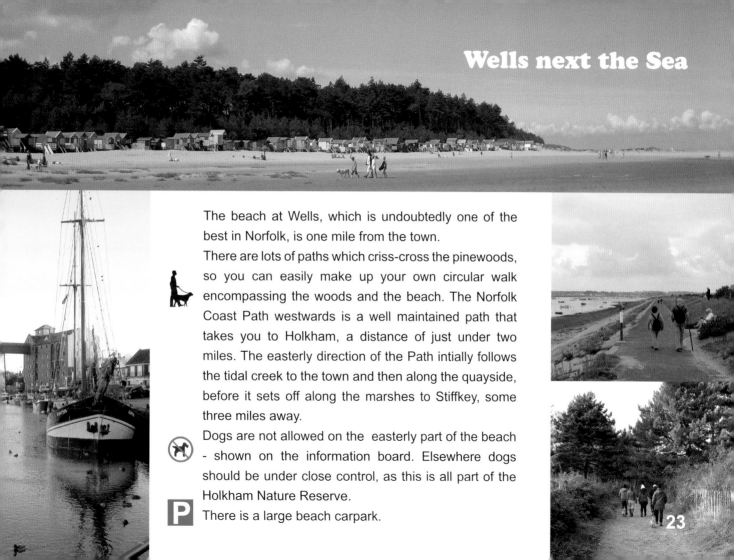

The beach at Wells, which is undoubtedly one of the best in Norfolk, is one mile from the town.

There are lots of paths which criss-cross the pinewoods, so you can easily make up your own circular walk encompassing the woods and the beach. The Norfolk Coast Path westwards is a well maintained path that takes you to Holkham, a distance of just under two miles. The easterly direction of the Path intially follows the tidal creek to the town and then along the quayside, before it sets off along the marshes to Stiffkey, some three miles away.

Dogs are not allowed on the easterly part of the beach - shown on the information board. Elsewhere dogs should be under close control, as this is all part of the Holkham Nature Reserve.

There is a large beach carpark.

Stiffkey

Red Lion
44 Wells Road NR23 1AJ
"No restrictions to customer
areas, water bowls and dog
nibbles provided free".
Covered outside area.

Stiffkey Stores
Wells Road NR23 1QH
"Dogs allowed inside if they
are carried or they can go
into one of our beach huts for
coffee and cake"
Note - the two mini beach
huts with tables and chairs
inside, can be seen in the
photograph.

The Stiffkey Saltmarsh, which is part of the Blakeney National Nature Reserve, is a maze of winding creeks with marshland plants such as sea aster and sea lavender.

There are clearly paths out into the marshes and bridges over the creeks, but we would not suggest that you explore unless you have a local guide.

A safer alternative is to stick to the Norfolk Coast Path which follows the edge of the marshes - eastwards to Morston ($2^3/_4$m) and westwards to Wells ($2^1/_4$m).

There is a small carpark at the end Green Way, which is a turning off the A149 at the western end of the village.

As this is part of the Blakeney National Nature Reserve dogs should be kept under close control.

25

An absolute must when you visit Morston is to take one of the many boat trips to see the seals at Blakeney Point. Jason Bean advised us that well behaved dogs on leads are allowed on his boats and we are sure this is true of the other operators. On some of the trips you are allowed ashore, but dogs are restricted to the area immediately around the lifeboat house.

The Norfolk Coast Path passes through Morston and so you have the choice of walking westwards towards Stiffkey, a total distance of some three miles if you go the whole way. Or you can travel eastwards towards Blakeney - a more manageable $1\frac{1}{2}$ miles.

Morston is situated on the tidal Morston Creek, popular with boat owners. There is no access to any beaches from here. There is a National Trust visitor centre with a lookout providing extensive views of the surrounding marshes. Hot drinks and snacks can be purchased from the centre and from a mobile seafood sandwich van which is often present in the summer.

 The large car park is free for National Trust members.

 Dogs should be kept under close control, as there are muddy creeks, marshes and wildfowl.

27

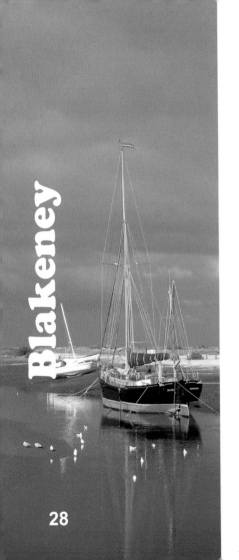

Blakeney

The King's Arms
Westgate Street NR25 7NQ
(Westgate Street is at at the western end of the quay - where the footpath to Morston starts)
"Dogs are allowed in the pub but strictly on a lead and not on the furniture."
Outdoor Tables

The Wiveton Bell
Blakeney Road Wiveton NR25 7TL (on the village green)
Take the turning off the A148 by Blakeney church and Wiveton is one mile down this road.
The website says "..people can wander in with walking boots and dogs to enjoy good company..."
Outdoor tables.

Blakeney is one of the most picturesque villages on the North Norfolk coast.

There is a large car park alongside the creek, where you can buy a crab sandwich in the summer and sit at the tables provided, while watching all the activity on the water. The car park is free for NT members.

There is no access to the beach from here, but there are two sections of the Norfolk Coast Path that you can walk along. From Morston to Blakeney (about $1^1/_2$ miles) The picture on the right shows this path with Blakeney in the distance. The easterly section starts at the car park and finishes at Cley-next-the-Sea, a distance of some $2^1/_2$ miles.

The George Hotel
High Street NR25 7RN
"Dogs are welcome in the bar and
the first half of the restaurant"
Large garden with tables.

Cookes of Cley
High Street NR25 7RX
"Dogs allowed as long as they are well
behaved, not too wet or muddy"
Outside tables.
Open daily in school holidays otherwise
(Friday) Saturday and Sunday

West Cottage Cafe
"We allow clean and dry dogs, but prefer not
to have them if everyone is eating lunch"
Outdoor tables - we provide water and dog
biscuits too. Closed on Fridays in the winter.

The Three Swallows
Newgate Green NR25 7TT
"Dogs on leads allowed throughout
the pub and garden areas"

The beach at Cley is the start of the four mile long spit that is the Blakeney Point.Nature Reserve To the east is the beach of a Norfolk Wild Life Trust Reserve.

 No dogs are permitted on Blakeney Point from the beginning of April to mid August, except for two dog walking areas near Cley beach and around the lifeboat house. Dogs are to be kept on a lead or under close control in these two areas.

 The photograph above is of the Norfolk Coast Path which you can join from the road to the west of Cley and is $1\frac{1}{2}$ miles to Blakeney, passing reed beds on your right.

 The beach car park is off the road to the east of Cley.

Muckleburgh Military Collection
Off the A149 NR25 7EG
You may like to see the largest privately owned military collection while you are at Weybourne. They accommodate visitors with dogs by providing sturdy pens with padlocks.

Kelling Heath
NR25 7HW
A campsite/holiday park set in 250 acres of woodland and rare open heathland in an area of outstanding natural beauty. A maximum of two dogs, which must be on a lead at all times and not left unattended

Emcy Garden Centre
Weybourne Road NR25 7ER
(On the Weybourne to Holt Road)
Well behaved dogs are allowed in the garden centre and in the cafe within the garden centre.

Weybourne is the point on the North Norfolk coast where the cliffs to the east meets the shingle beach which stretches westwards.

You can walk westwards along the beach, but we find it hard work walking on the shingle, although this is the route if you are following the Norfolk Coast Path. Eastwards the Coast Path rises with the cliffs and extends for three miles to Sheringham, although after only one mile you have the option to follow a path inland to the Sheringham Country Park (page 34).

We can also recommend walks on Kelling Heath, which is reached from the Holiday Park entrance on the Weybourne to Holt Road. Kelling Heath is 250 acres of woodland and rare open heathland. There are several woodland walks and nature trails, for which leaflets can be obtained from the visitor centre.

There is a large carpark at Weybourne beach.

Sheringham Country Park (on the A148) is one of our favourite places for walking our dogs. It is owned by the National Trust and while it is not quite on the coast, it qualifies to be in the book because you can see the sea from a number of vantage points and there is a path which takes you to the Norfolk Coast Path on the cliff top between Sheringham and Weybourne (crossing the A149). Sheringham Park is famous for its rhododendrons and azaleas which attract visitors from far and wide. There is a courtyard with tables where purchased drinks and snacks can be consumed and dogs are permitted.

There are miles of waymarked walks, some are firm and others are natural paths through the wooded areas. You can extend your walk to Weybourne station and then on into Kelling Heath.

For the most part dogs are allowed off the lead, provided they are under control ie. will respond immediately when called. There are clearly marked areas where your dog must be on a lead - around the car park and visitor centre and in the parkland when cattle are grazing.

The car park is free for National Trust members.

Sheringham

The Funky Mackerel Cafe
Cliff Road PE31 8AP
Between the carpark and promenade
"Well behaved dogs on leads"
Outdoor tables
Winter opening Thursday - Sunday

Ellie's Beachside Café
West promenade
"Dogs are allowed without restriction"
Outdoor tables
Open mid March to end October

Whelk Coppers Tea Rooms
25 The Driftway NR26 8LD
Dogs are allowed inside
without restriction
Outdoor tables overlooking seafront

Sheringham

Sheringham claims to be North Norfolk's premier seaside town and there is no doubt that it has many delightful attributes for visitors, both by the sea and within the town.

There are several car parks in Sheringham. There is a large one by the steam railway station, where they also hold markets. For easy access to the beach and promenade the Cliff Road car park has steps directly down to the promenade and beach. There is also some parking on the western side, by the model boat pool. This is the best place if you are wanting to walk westwards past the golf course along the Norfolk Coast Path.

Sheringham

The Two Lifeboats
2 High Street NR26 8JR
"Dogs are allowed on the ground floor of the premises only at out of season times"
Outdoor tables.

The Windham Arms
15 Wyndham Street NR26 8BA
"Dogs are allowed in the bar side of the restaurant and in the public bar"
Outdoor tables

Dunstable Arms
27 Cromer Road NR26 8AB
"Dogs are allowed in the bar and garden lounge if you are eating"
Outdoor tables

The Coffee House Café
8 Station Approach NR26 8RA
Two tables are provided inside for dogs.
Outdoor tables - water provided

Sheringham

At low tide it is pleasant to walk along the beach either westwards to Weybourne or eastwards to West Runton. If you are more energetic you can take the cliff top paths following the Norfolk Coast Path. Westwards you climb to a peak as you walk alongside Sheringham golf course and at the top you have spectacular views as far as Blakeney Point. If you choose to walk in an easterly direction you have an even steeper climb to the top of Beeston Bump, from where you can see Cromer church and lighthouse in the distance. You can walk to West Runton and return along the beach making a three mile round trip.

Dogs are banned from the beach at Sheringham from 1 May to 30 September. The area of exclusion corresponds with the length of the promenade and just beond the furthest groynes. On the paths and promenade they must be on a lead no more than 1.8 metres long.

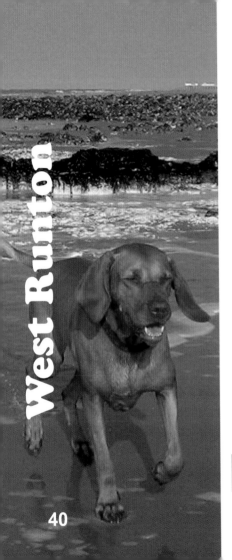

West Runton

The Village Inn
Water Lane NR27 9QP
"Dogs are allowed inside"
Large south facing walled garden
- dogs allowed on leads
Open all year

The Beach Café
At the beach end of Water Lane
Dogs are allowed inside
Louise the proprietor is very dog
friendly - she owns a Hungarian
Vislar, see picture left.
Outdoor tables with great views
of the sea.

Beeston Regis Holiday Park
Cromer Road NR27 9QZ
Dogs Welcome
www.beestonregis.co.uk

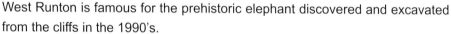

West Runton

West Runton is famous for the prehistoric elephant discovered and excavated from the cliffs in the 1990's.

There is a large grassy cliff top car park located close to the beach.

You can walk along the beach eastwards to East Runton and to Sheringham in the opposite direction - taking care to avoid high water and the risk of being cut off. There is a cliff top path which takes you all the way to Sheringham ($1\frac{1}{2}$ miles), you can walk around the 64metre high Beeston Bump, if you can't summon the energy to climb over it. The eastwards path doesn't extend all the way on the cliff top to East Runton, but ultimately brings you to the A149 coast road as it enters the village.

If you are staying in the area of West Runton, you should discover the many paths just inland of the village, including the last section of the Norfolk Coast Path to Cromer, which turned inland at Beeston Regis.

East Runton

White Horse
High Street NR27 9NX
"Dogs are welcome but must be kept
quiet and under control"
Outside Tables

Woodhill Park
Cromer Road NR27 9PX
"Dogs only permitted on touring
pitches booked on the designated
touring pitch dog area. Dogs must be
on a lead at all times and must not be
left unattended, Dogs are not permitted in lodges and holiday hire homes"
www.woodhill-park.com

Manor Farm
NR27 9PR
"Dogs to be kept on short leads"
www.manorfarmcaravansite.co.uk

The view from Manor Farm

East Runton is a very popular holiday village with many caravan parks and campsites.

You can walk along the beach to West Runton and to Cromer - this is best done at low tide when the sand becomes quite firm. You cannot walk along the cliff top here, the Norfolk Coast Path passes from West Runton to Cromer on the landward side of East Runton village. If you have the time you should explore the many paths beyond East Runton's Top Common, particularly the one that takes you to the top of Ingleborough Hill.

There is a carpark at the top of the slope that leads down to the beach.

There are no restrictions on dogs on the beach at East Runton, but please be aware that this beach can be very busy in the summer.

43

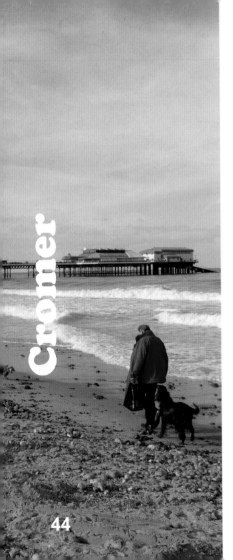

Rocket House Café
The Gangway East Promenade
NR27 9ET
The Rocket House has great views of
the sea - dogs are not allowed inside,
but they are allowed on the balcony -
one part of which is behind glass.

Red Lion
Brook Street NR27 9HD
(You cannot see it in this photograph
but the Red Lion overlooks the sea)
"Dogs are allowed in all areas except the
restaurant, but we do serve food where
owners are allowed to sit with dogs.
Dogs are allowed to stay in the hotel."

Forest Park Caravan Site
Northrepps Road NR27 0JR
Dogs are welcome - to be kept on leads
at all times
www.forest-park.co.uk

Cromer is the quintessential seaside town which describes itself as the Gem of the Norfolk Coast.

There are two carparks within the town, but the best for access to the beach and to a large grass area, is the cliff top Runton Road carpark. This is directly off the coast road as you enter Cromer from East Runton.

Dogs are banned from the main beaches in Cromer from 1st May to 30th September. Information boards show the area of the exclusion, but for the most part it corresponds with the extent of the promenade.

On the promenade and paths dogs must be kept on a lead which is no more than 1.8m long.

45

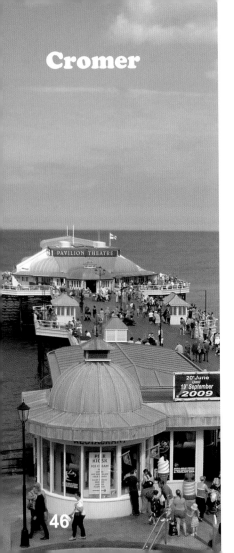

Cromer

Blue Sky Cafe
Runton Road NR27 9AV
(By the cliff top Runton Road carpark)
"Well behaved dogs allowed inside"
Outdoor tables
Long weekend opening in winter

The Albion
32 Church Street NR27 9ES
"Dogs welcome, no restrictions, water
available on request"

The Old Rock Shop Bistro
10 Hamilton Road NR27 9HL
Dogs welcome providing they are well
behaved and kept at ground level

Deer's Glade Camping
& Caravan Park
White Post Road
Hanworth NR11 7HN
Dogs Welcome
www. deersglade.co.uk

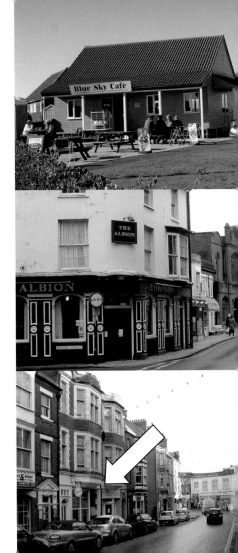

Beyond the excluded section of beach you can walk eastwards to Overstrand and westwards to East Runton. At low water more firm sand is exposed, which our dogs particularly enjoy - especially when chasing a ball.

There is no cliff top path between Cromer and East Runton, but we can recommend discovering the path in the other direction. This rises with the cliff out of Cromer (top right), starting off as a fully made path and then becoming a track right up to the lighthouse. This is the start of the Paston Way. As you ascend, you pass woods on your right, through which there are a number of paths and then an open area known as Happy Valley. Over the summit the path continue with a golf course to your right and the cliffs to your left. The total distance to Overstrand is around two miles, you can take refreshment in the Cliff Top Cafe and then return along the beach.

Overstrand

The Cliff Top Café
22 Cliff Road NR27 0PP
(Excellent view of the sea)
"Dogs are most welcome
- on a lead please"
Outdoor tables
Closed through January and
on Mondays and Tuesdays
in the winter.

The White Horse
34 High Street NR27 0AB
"Dogs are allowed in the bar,
gardens and some guest rooms"
Outdoor tables.

Overstrand is a pleasant coastal village made famous in the late 1800's through the writings of Clement Scott, the drama critic of the Daily Telegraph.

The beach is good for walking with dogs at low water - westward takes you to Cromer and eastwards to Trimingham - both are about two miles away.

You can walk westwards along the cliff top to Cromer - the path leaves directly from the cliff top car park and for the most part you have the golf course on your left and the sea on your right. This path is the first section of the Paston Way. Heading eastwards from Overstrand the Paston Way takes you inland, south of Trimingham, before bringing you back to the coast at Mundesley.

There is a pay and display cliff top car park.

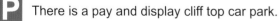

Dogs are banned from the central part of beach in Overstrand from 1st May to 30th September. The exclusion area corresponds with the length of the promenade. On the promenade dogs must be kept on a lead no more than 1.8m long.

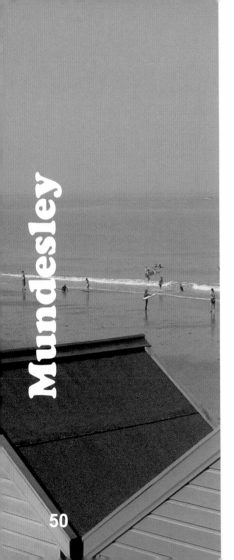

The Ship Inn
21 Beach Road NR11 8BQ
"Dogs are allowed in the front bar
on a lead at all times"
Outdoor tables

Jonet Restaurant
17 Beach Road NR11 8BG
"Dogs are allowed in the
restaurant on specific tables"
Outside tables
Reduced opening hours
November to Easter
9-2 Friday to Monday

The Corner House Café
2-4 Cromer Road NR11 8BE
"Dogs are allowed inside and
made welcome with dog treats"
Outdoor tables
Closed on Mondays in the winter.

Mundesley is a large village located at a dip in the cliffs on the B1159. There is a wide firm beach at low water, ideal for dog walking. Westwards it is almost three miles to Trimingham, but there is a slope up the cliffs to the west side of Mundesley after one mile. Eastwards along the beach takes you to Bacton ($2\frac{1}{2}$m), this is actually a section of the Paston Way. Halfway along there is the opportunity to walk inland to Paston. The westwards section of the Paston Way takes you inland to Gimingham, which is just under two miles.

There is a carpark on the opposite side of the road to the beach access slope.

Dogs are banned from the central part of the beach in Mundesley from 1st May to 30th September. The exclusion area corresponds with the length of the promenade. On the promenade dogs must be kept on a lead no more than 1.8m long.

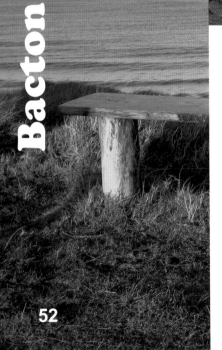

The beach at Bacton is wide and firm at low water, but is mostly covered at high tide. Behind the beach is a concrete sea defence with a wide apron that acts as a promenade and extends for the full distance of the Bacton sea frontage. Above this is a grassy embankment along which there is also a footpath. There are several beach access points. Westwards along the beach takes you to Mundesley ($2^{1}/_{2}$ m) or half way you can walk inland to Paston - the beach route corresponds with a section of the Paston Way. Eastwards along the beach takes you past Keswick to Walcott ($1^{1}/_{2}$ m). The Paston Way continues inland for six miles to North Walsham where it ends, but where you can link in to the Weaver's Way. A popular area for walking dogs within a short drive from Bacton is Bacton Wood (also known as Witton Wood) it is owned by the Forestry Commission and part managed by North Norfolk District Council. You take the B1150 North Walsham road and turn left after two miles - there are parking areas within the wood.

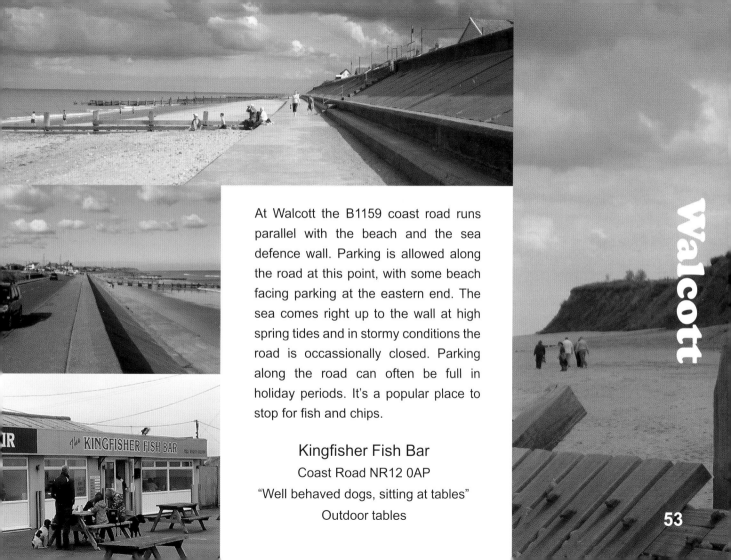

At Walcott the B1159 coast road runs parallel with the beach and the sea defence wall. Parking is allowed along the road at this point, with some beach facing parking at the eastern end. The sea comes right up to the wall at high spring tides and in stormy conditions the road is occassionally closed. Parking along the road can often be full in holiday periods. It's a popular place to stop for fish and chips.

Kingfisher Fish Bar
Coast Road NR12 0AP
"Well behaved dogs, sitting at tables"
Outdoor tables

Smallsticks Barn Café
Cart gap Road NR12 0QL
"Dogs are not allowed in the
cafe but in the large enclosed
courtyard area, with an outside
tap and dog bowls"
Closed Mondays
Open weekends in winter
(November to Easter)
Below - access to the beach at
Cart Gap

Happisburgh

Happisburgh is the Norfolk village that has been most affected by cliff erosion, many properties have been lost and various beach access steps and ramps have been built and subsequently lost. At the time of writing a new ramp has been created down to the beach from Happisburgh village (and a new carpark). However when we are walking in this area, we prefer to park at a car park one mile to the east of Happisburgh, at Cart Gap. There are no cliffs at this point and access to the beach is simple.

At low water the sand is firm and you can walk westwards to Walcott ($1\frac{1}{2}$ m from Happisburgh) or eastwards past Eccles-on-Sea to Sea Palling - just under three miles from Cart Gap. There are a number of inland paths, one from Happisburgh to Lessingham and another from Eccles to Hempstead.

Sea Palling

Reefs Bar
Beach Road NR12 0AL
"Dogs are allowed anywhere in the pub on a lead"
Large patio area with water bowls and a dog treat machine.
Open all year.

The Old Hall Inn
The Street NR12 0TZ
"Dogs are permitted in the main bar, the family room bar, but not in the restaurant"
Outdoor tables

Sea Palling has a huge sandy bay with a fine beach backed by sand dunes. This superb beach has come about because of a beach reclamation and sea defence scheme, involving the construction of nine reefs just offshore. These have allowed the sand to build up into bays. As a result it is a very popular destination in the summer, but it is also popular throughout the year with dog owners. On a bright winter's day - as shown above - there can be few better places to be. Along the beach you can walk westwards for three miles to Happisburgh or eastwards for one mile to Waxham.

There is a large beach car park from where there is easy access to the beach.

Waxham

There is an access path to the beach through the high sand dunes from the small village of Waxham on the B1159. There is no official parking, just a limited amount of unofficial road-side parking in the lane leading to the beach access. Consequently the beach is sparsely populated even at peak times. Nearby is the Waxham Great Barn, which is the longest in Norfolk and was built in the 1580's. You can walk along the beach westwards for one mile to Sea Palling, or eastwards for two miles to Warren Farm campsite and then Horsey Gap just beyond.

Waxham Barn Café
Coast Road NR12 0DY
"Dogs are allowed in the courtyard on a lead, not in the cafe"

Horsey Gap is an access point to the beach through a ridge of high sand dunes, from the coast road just to the west of the village of Horsey. There is a wide sandy beach, which is becoming increasingly well known for its seals. From November a colony of Grey seals give birth to their single white pups on the beach. At this time the beach is roped off and a viewing platform is provided, so you can observe the seals at close quarters.

 You can walk eastwards along the beach for one mile and then take a path inland to the village of Horsey - a further mile. You can complete the walk continuing inland. There is also a footpath alongside Horsey Mere, which is part of the Norfolk Broads. The area is the Horsey Warren nature reserve and you must keep off the sand dunes. Dogs must of course be kept away from the seals.

P There is a pay and display carpark at Horsey Gap and a National Trust carpark at Horsey Mill on Horsey Mere.

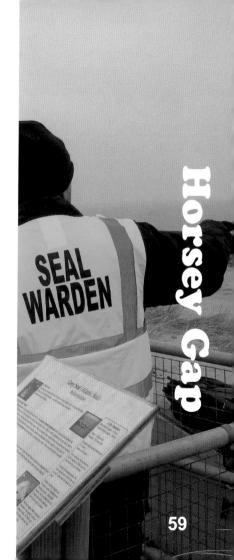

Horsey Gap

Winterton on Sea

60

Winterton Dunes Beach Café

Beach Road NR29 4AJ

"Dogs are not allowed inside but are welcome at the tables outside, where there are rings to tie the dogs and water and chews are provided. Weekends only from end October to end January (Open Boxing Day to New Year's Day inclusive)

The extensive sandy beach at Winterton is backed by high sand dunes and a large area of dune heath and grasslands that extends to Horsey, forming the Winterton Dunes National Nature Reserve. The area is designated as a Site of Special Scientific interest with a wide range of species, including the Natterjack toad and a 110 species of moths.

Paths criss-cross the dune heath and are particulalry good for walking in the winter, as they remain firm and dry even after heavy rain and they are sheltered from the cold winds that can hit this north-east corner of the Norfolk Coast.

Given that it is a nature reserve, dogs should be kept under close control. Avoid the high sand dunes, with the possibility of nesting birds and be aware of seals that may have strayed from Horsey.

There is a beach side carpark from which there is also direct access to the grasslands.

Acknowledgements
We would like to thank the friends
and family who have allowed us
to use their photographs of their
dogs in this book.

Laura Hughes
Will Appleyard
Louise O'Shea
Caroline Chilvers

We would also like to thank and
acknowledge -

The Holkham Estate
The National Trust

and Barbara, Suzie & Daisy

Printed by Barnwell Print Ltd,
Aylsham, Norfolk

The Beach Code and the Coastal Code

Please remember the following key points from the above two published codes.

- Try to leave everything as you found it.
- Clean up after your dog.
- Keep your dog under tight control. Wildlife, livestock and other people can feel threatened by dogs and it is illegal to disturb or harass many species of birds and other animals.
- Avoid sand dunes, saltmarsh and cliffs - they are sensitive environments and vulnerable to erosion.
- Keep to established footpaths and boardwalks. Tread carefully on the shoreline to avoid damaging rockpools and marine life. Respect our coastline and other users.
- Avoid disturbing wintering birds during cold spells - at these times they must feed whenever possible and conserve their energy.

Steve and Alyson Appleyard live on the North Norfolk coast with their Norfolk Terriers, Archie and Rosie.

Also by Steve & Alyson Appleyard

Norfolk Beaches

This book shows every one of Norfolk's 50 unique beaches along its ninety miles of coastline, from the remote to the popular. Illustrated with 550 photographs 128 pages ISBN 978-0-9561346-0-8   £9.99

Suffolk Beaches

A guide to the 34 beaches and shores of the 47 miles of the Suffolk coastline each with its own unique character. Illustrated with 220 photographs 128 pages ISBN 978-0-9561346-2-2   £9.99

Children' Norfolk & Suffolk

Shows the best 100 places to visit in Norfolk and Suffolk with a further thirty things to do. Illustrated with more than 500 photographs 160 pages ISBN 978-0-9561346-1-5   £9.99